To. Sofia.
You are very
special, one of a kind.
Daughter of the King of ♡!
never give up!
lots of love
Jenny

RUN YOUR OWN RACE!

Run Your Own Race!: Practical Tips for Running Well
By Jeanny Rodriguez

2019 © Jeanny Rodriguez

ISBN-13: 978-1733174701
ISBN-10: 1733174702

Edited by Rachel Newman

Commissioned by:
The King's Company
Odessa, Texas

Published by:
Lazarus Tribe Media, LLC
Rome, Georgia

RUN YOUR OWN RACE!

PRACTICAL TIPS FOR RUNNING WELL

BY JEANNY RODRIGUEZ

THE KING'S COMPANY
ODESSA, TEXAS

Lazarus Tribe Media
Rome, Georgia

My joy and my strength come from Jesus Christ, to Him I give all praise and gratitude. Thank you, Mom, for your unquestionable love and support. For having us twins in your small body and never giving up. In memory, I dedicate this work to my loving twin sister, Hildi & my daughter, Adriana. 'Til we meet again and we can run together & forever through the streets of gold in Heaven! Shalom.

CONTENTS

12.1 DECLARATION

I DECLARE:

Let it be, today, that I am made to run my own race.

I am not alone.

I am surrounded by the best.

I will leave everything that is holding me back,
and I will run away from everyday sin.

I will not give up.

I will not give in.

I will keep running my own race,

the one created just for me,

Staying in my lane to the finish line.

I keep my eyes on Jesus and I win!

12.1

THE BIRTH OF 12.1 RUN YOUR OWN RACE

My Big Crash

My identical twin sister was diagnosed with lung cancer on December 24, 2011.

I fell down hard. Never before had my life come to such a screeching halt.

Not after my daughter died.

Not after my divorce.

Not even after my two times being diagnosed with cancer.

The news of her diagnosis came one month after I had gotten married for the second time. I fell on my knees, cried out to God as hard as I could, and I said, "I'm done. I'm done running away from you. Take it all, take me, I am done. I'm all in!"

This was my big fall. I finally crashed. But I decided to stop hiding from Him.

I put my sight on Jesus and I started running towards Him. It wasn't easy.

Sometimes I couldn't get out of bed. Some days, I couldn't breathe. Some days I couldn't eat or walk, but I knew I had to, so I crawled.

My sister passed away October 15, 2012. It took me a while, but I knew I had to keep putting one foot in front of the other.

On January 7, 2018, I declared that I would do a Daniel fast for 21 days. What was I thinking?! It was soooo hard to do, but so worth it. Well, guess what happened... Heaven opened up, yes it did! And things started happening.

During that time, I kept hearing in my heart, "Run your own race." When I would talk to different friends and people that I met, they would ask me how I had made it this far with everything that had happened in my life. I would find myself saying, "By God's grace and running my own race, and you need to run your own race, too!"

Faith Requires Action!

In late April 2018, I met a lady, and while talking to her I had the impression that she was a runner. So, I asked her, and she responded, "Yes, how did you know?" and went on to tell me how she started running.

She said that she began running at 62-years-young, and that was 10 years ago!

She has run several races, including a 26.2 marathon and two 13.1 half-marathons. She went on to inform me that earlier that year she had been in an accident (not her fault) and totaled her car. Moreso than losing the car, losing all her original race stickers upset her greatly! She specifically told me that she was going to order replacements, including a "13.1" half-marathon sticker.

The word "sticker" and the number *stuck* in my mind. I could not stop thinking about that sticker!

The next day I went for an airboat ride. While zooming fast over alligators, the number "12.1" flashed in my head! I thought it was very strange and immediately asked God, "What is that?" But I didn't hear anything.

So I went on about my day, and the day after that, and the day after that... On that rainy evening while driving I asked again, "What is 12.1, God?"

He said, "Hebrews, Look up Hebrews 12:1." And there it was!

12.1 Run Your Own Race was born!

12.1 is Life's Race.

Remember, the 12 disciples and 1 Son of God, Jesus.

The "point"? It is finished at the Cross!

The oval? We are never alone! We are surrounded by a GREAT cloud of witnesses watching over us always.

You see, God's got it, He set up this life's race. It is all a set-up! Jesus holds your right hand and He is running with you! Never give up! Run Your Own Life's Race! You will win and finish your race well! Don't look back, let's keep our eyes on Jesus, and WE WIN! Heaven is our destination, our home forever and ever.

All for the Glory of God!

So get out there and RUN YOUR OWN RACE!

Jeanny

RECEIVE & RUN WITH JESUS

Win eternal life, forever and ever?

Life is the Best Race you can ever win! To have eternal life... THAT IS THE WINNING PRIZE!

The most important relationship of your life is a personal relationship with Jesus Christ. If you would like to receive Him as your Lord and Savior, and enter into the greatest relationship you have ever known, please pray the prayer below.

> *Father,*
>
> *You loved the world so much that You gave Your only begotten Son to die for our sins so that whoever believes in You will not perish but have eternal life.*
>
> *Your Word says we are saved by grace through faith as a gift from You. There is nothing we can do to earn salvation.*
>
> *I believe and confess with my mouth what Jesus Christ is Your Son, The Savior of the world. I believe He died on the cross for me and bore all of my sins, paying the price for me.*
>
> *I believe in my heart that You raised Jesus from the dead and that He is alive today.*
>
> *I am a sinner, and I am sorry for my sins, and I ask You to forgive me. By faith, I receive Jesus Christ now as my Lord and Savior.*
>
> *I believe that I am saved and will spend eternity with YOU! Thank you, Father. I am so grateful for your salvation.*
>
> *In Jesus' Name, Amen!*

WELCOME TO THE FAMILY!

SIGN UP FOR THE RACE
Make Your Commitment

Fast track tips:
Make a decision to run
Have determination to run well

Are you ready to run your life's race? You have a race marked for you, only you! I want to encourage you today to sign up for the race!

Guys! I was sooo happy to learn that I am one of a kind! ...especially since I came into this world as twin sister. Ugh! We were compared to each other all the time... not good! She didn't like it and I hated it. Ahhhh!

BUT, I have my own life's race! Thank youuuuu, God! So, I get ready to run my race everyday. I get up with awe and wonder of what God has in store for me each day.

I pray you guys get ready to run your own race, too! Now, GO! Run it!

You are one of a kind!

You are awesome!

You are unique!

What are you waiting for? Make the decision to run today!

"You saw me before I was born. Every day of my life was recorded in your book. Every moment was laid out before a single day had passed."
- Psalm 139:16 NLT

Race Reflections:

Did you enjoy running races as a child? What do you enjoy about your life today?
Do you believe God wants you to take pleasure in running your life's race for Him?

COACH

The Father, the Son, and the Holy Spirit

Fast Track Tips:
Get to know your Coach well
Listen to your Coach
Always ask questions when you have them

You are growing in God, and He is so pleased with you!!! Our great Coach has given you everything you need to fulfill your life's race--to fulfill His will right where you are. And though He will continually grow, stretch, and mold you, you don't have to wait until His work in you is completed to live in the destiny for which He created you. As your Coach, the Father will teach you how to set your pace in this race so you can run with endurance.

When during your race you find yourself in the middle of loss, pain, or difficult circumstances, allow your Coach to strengthen and motivate you. He helps us flourish in a close relationship with Him. Jesus Himself gave everything for us. He lived this life and paid with His life so we can live forever. He ran the good race... and He won!

"If you need wisdom, ask our generous God, and he will give it to you. He will not rebuke you for asking. But when you ask him, be sure that your faith is in God alone. Do not waver, for a person with divided loyalty is as unsettled as a wave of the sea that is blown and tossed by the wind." - James 1:5-6 NLT

The Holy Spirit is also GREAT Helper to us. When we don't know how to pray, He prays for us. He works in our life's race. He goes ahead of us and makes our race lanes straight. He remains in us, He confronts us, helps us, guides us, teaches us, comes alongside us, comforts us, and intercedes and advocates for us. There is no area in which we won't need him in our life's race. Call on Him and you will see how He shows up and shows off. He will go ahead of us and help us in this Life's marathon race.

"But when the Father sends the Advocate as my representative--that is, the Holy Spirit--he will teach you everything and will remind you of everything I have told you." - John 14:26 NLT

Race Reflections:

How well do you know your Coach? How well have you let Him get to know you?

TRAINING
Preparing for an Eternal Prize

Fast Track Tips:
Mental Stamina
Physical (Nutritional) Endurance
Spiritual Discipline

What type of training do you need to run your life's race? Mental, Physical, and Spiritual training are a must.

You must be diligent about what you allow your mind to focus on. You must take care of your physical body and be mindful of your nutritional needs. And you must allow your spirit to be disciplined and trained by the Spirit of God.

As you run your own race you will be stretched mentally, physically, and spiritually. This develops endurance and perseverance to carry you through the race.

Give the race your all! You are going to want to give up at times, but don't!

As an example, on those days that I have a hard time getting up, I play a little game. I set a timer for 15 minutes. In those 15 minutes, I run to beat the clock! For 15 minutes I run to make my bed, and hang up clothes or throw them in the laundry basket. Then, I jump in the shower and brush my teeth. This "run to beat the clock game" gives me a huge win to get things going for the day! Even if that's all I get done in my day, I accomplish quite a bit!

In the end, it will all be worth it. God has marked out your race. So keep your eyes on the finish line, on Jesus, and you will win!

"All athletes are disciplined in their training. They do it to win a prize that will fade away, but we do it for an eternal prize." - 1 Corinthians 9:25 NLT

Race Reflections:

In what areas of your life would you like to receive more training?
What is one thing you can do today to pursue those goals?

RUNNER
Your Heavenly Identity

Fast Track Tips:
Embrace your inner runner
Understand why you are running

You are the runner in this life's marathon race. Trust me, the race will get hard! I've walked through cancer, twice! I've experienced divorce...also, times two! Sure, there have been many other difficulties come my way. Every time, the one thing that I could count on for sure was that I could run to God. And run to Him I did!

Running as hard as I could to my Coach was my safety net. I kept holding to His promises, the Word, His Word. I read that He would always hold me up and give me the strength to go through any storm. He is not a small shack by the beach, He is strong fortress!!! When I run to Jesus, I know that I am safe and strong in His arms for sure!

Oh yes, I have been weak! So many times I was quick to fall apart, fall into negativity, or run to the people that were even more broken than me. I learned during my life's race that I must run to my Dad, the King of kings and Lord of lords. He never leaves me nor forsakes me. He is crazy about me! He holds my right hand and never lets go. He is my strength.

"The name of the Lord is a strong fortress; the godly run to him and are safe." - Proverbs 18:10 NLT

"...I will hold you up with my victorious right hand." - Isaiah 41:10 NLT

Race Reflections:

Who and/or what keeps you motivated to run your race?
What is one way you run to God when the race becomes difficult?

TEAM
Your Kingdom Family

Fast track tips:
Learn to help others with your strengths
Learn to get help from your team in your weaknesses

When I think of my favorite team, I see the 12 Disciples–12 buddies, the guys that walked the Earth with King Jesus. They were 12 chosen men, all different. They were so imperfect, broken, sinners, but they chose to follow this Jesus when He called them.

They all walked together and helped each other out. They each had their own strengths and abilities. Every one of them had a one-of-a-kind life's race (some turned out better than others, for sure), but they ran together and changed history! They persevered as a team, kept their eyes on Jesus, and won their races!

That is exactly what we need to do in order for us to run the race marked out for us and win. Get a team. Get like-minded people around you to help you persevere. And remember, you can help others run their races, too!

"This makes for harmony among the members, so that all the members care for each other. If one part suffers, all the parts suffer with it, and if one part is honored, all the parts are glad. All of you together are Christ's body, and each of you is a part of it." - 1 Corinthians 12:25-27 NLT

Race Reflections:

What do you think is your greatest strength? Your weakness?
With who in your community are you currently
sharing your strengths and weaknesses?

RELAY RACE
Serving Each Other

Fast track tips:
Stay in your lane & stick to the plan
Do not get distracted
Help others

How can we help each other in our life's race?

A relay race is a race between teams of two or more contestants with each team member covering a specified portion of the entire course. Your life's race will look much like a relay race at times--you need someone other than yourself to run your race well.

More than anything now, in this social media world, it's important to have connections with other people. We all need community with family and friends. One of our very basic needs is to belong. Even when God created Adam, He said it was not good for Adam to be alone.

The symbol "12.1" is a reminder of the 12 disciples that walked with Jesus. Twelve, teenage buddies walking together with Jesus. I'm sure it wasn't easy, and I'm sure they were always hungry...you know how teenagers are! They were not perfect, but they stuck together.

Take time out of your life's race to connect with others, pray for your friends, and sit with family that are going through pain or loss. A simple smile or a hug, especially when we're going through difficult times, is super-needed!

Keep it simple. Show up with a listening ear or a dish of food. And allow others to show up for you as well. There is powerful simplicity in being blessed by and being a blessing to others.

"Bear one another's burdens, and so fulfill the law of Christ."
- Galatians 6:2 ESV

Race Reflections:

What is your favorite way to serve someone else?
What is your favorite way for someone to serve you?

RACE TRACK/COURSE
Proper Preparation

Fast Track Tips:
Map out your race
Plan your steps

Do you really control your life?

We all try to control our lives. We plan daily activities, plan our meals, plan what we're going to wear, but we never know what's coming just around the corner! What happens when three things we manage well turn into six things to conquer? And then those six things turn into nine things we are barely able to handle? What happens then?

We must trust God with everything! No matter how much we attempt to control every step of our life's race, the next stride may surprise us.

Planning and preparing are not bad things. However, there is only so much you can plan for, and with the rest you're going to have to trust God! God has HIS great plans for you. He guides you wherever you go. He lights up your path. You can stay in step with Him for your entire race!

> *"The LORD directs the steps of the godly. He delights in every detail of their lives. Though they stumble, they will never fall, for the LORD holds them by the hand." - Psalm 37:23-24 NLT*

Race Reflections:

Have you struggled with trying to control everything in your life?
Are you willing today to trust God with the next steps of your race?

OBSTACLES
Facing Challenges

Fast Track Tips:
Expect opposition/hurdles
Plan ahead for victory

Here is a tough question to ask yourself: Are you always expecting the worse? Why?

Why even get up when the day is going to be awful?

Listen! Do you want to hear the truth? In life there is no way to avoid every obstacle and never need to clear some hurdles. But no matter how difficult your day may seem, God will give you the joy, the strength, and the peace you need to get through it.

Simply focus on one win at a time. You only need to overcome the one obstacle directly in front of you. Listen to God. Listen more, talk less. Daydream and think with God. Surround yourself with like-minded people who will help you understand and fly over your hurdles. Accountability will accelerate the results you want.

As you win everyday battles, you will be able go higher and faster to the victory God has prepared for you. Pray and play. Rest and run your life's race. Victory is ahead one day at a time.

> *"Dear brothers and sisters, when troubles come your way, consider it an opportunity for great joy. For you know that when your faith is tested, your endurance has a chance to grow. So let it grow, for when your endurance is fully developed, you will be perfect and complete, needing nothing."*
> *- James 1:2-4 NLT*

Race Reflections:

What is one big hurdle you are willing to release to God today, and let Him help you clear it?

WATER STATIONS
Rest and Stillness

Fast Track Tips:
Get poured into
Stay refreshed

Staying hydrated in life is super-important, especially when you're running. As you run, your body sweats and you have to increase your water intake.

During your life's race, you may have to walk, slow down, pace yourself...you don't know how far or how long is your race. One thing is certain, our races are marathons, not sprints.

When we run without staying hydrated and without resting, we get sick. We break down. With no rest we are a mess, short-tempered, and exhausted.

Do you want to be healthy? Don't be in a hurry to finish the race. Remember, this is a race everyone wins as they run WELL. Pacing yourself is key.

When you rest you will restore, replenish, refresh, reconnect, and rebuild yourself. So now, go for a walk, drink water, and close your eyes for 10-20 minutes.

Oh, and best of all! Did you know your rest is form of worship?! God loves it!

"Let my soul be at rest again, for the LORD has been good to me."
- Psalm 116:7 NLT

Race Reflections:

What is your favorite thing to do for rest? When is the last time you did that? Can you make time to do it today?

AUDIENCE/CHEERING FANS
Gifts from Above

Fast Track Tip:
Learn how to receive encouragement
Escape false humility

Take the gift! When someone says, *"You look pretty," "You are so smart," "I love your outfit," "I love your hair!"* listen up! Say, *"THANK YOU!"* Train yourself to receive encouragement even when you don't "feel" like what you're being told is true.

A compliment is a gift! Would you ever return a birthday gift back to the giver? When you return the compliment with, *"Not really," "This old thing?", "I bought it for $3,"* or *"I hate my hair,"* you are returning the gift with false humility. False humility devalues you and the person encouraging you! ESCAPE false humility today once and for all.

Father, forgive us, help us receive gifts from You and others today and always.

"Dear brothers and sisters, I close my letter with these last words: Be joyful. Grow to maturity. Encourage each other. Live in harmony and peace. Then the God of love and peace will be with you." - 2 Corinthians 13:11 NLT

Race Reflections:

What is the kindest encouragement you've ever received? How did it make you feel?

(12.1)

11

WINNING YOUR RACE
Walking in Victory

Fast Track Tips:
Maintain confidence
Lead from experience
Share your testimony

Spoiler alert! Life's race has no shortcuts. You are going through a season, not a sentence. You have to go through the process to get to the promise!

There is great reward for going through the process. You will grow confidence in God and how He marked your race from the beginning of time. You will begin to lead with experience, knowing your calling is inside you!

How do we win? By keeping our eyes on Jesus. There is no other way, period! He ran the most amazing race. He listened to His Great Coach/Father, trained, and stayed in His lane. He followed all the steps in His life's race and He won salvation at the cross for us. Thank God, He never gave up, and He kept going with passion and perseverance until the end.

As you run in victory, you have a responsibility to share your story. Don't be selfish and withhold your gift from others! You will bless others with your one-of-a-kind story. There is victory in and from your story. Others will receive breakthrough when you share the testimony of your amazing race!

"And they have conquered him by the blood of the Lamb and by the word of their testimony, for they loved not their lives even unto death."
- Revelation 12:11 ESV

Race Reflections:

In what have you gained experience during your race that you could share with others? Who is one person you can think of that would be encouraged by hearing your testimony?

THE FINISH LINE
Winning Together

Fast Track Tips:
Press on to the finish line
Celebrate together

We must leave everything behind that stumps us, trips us, holds us back, and gets in the way between us and Jesus.

Do you want to get your prize and win? Then you have to leave sin behind you and walk away! Now! There is no other way...

Did you know:

In your life's race you are surrounded at all times by a great cloud of witnesses. Not a small cloud, but a GREAT cloud of witnesses. Our witnesses are all the previous saints that have passed! Great men and women of faith such as David, Jacob, Abraham, Esther, Debra, Mary, Rebekah... They see all our ups and downs, all our trials and tribulations, and they cheer us on! They celebrate our wins. They celebrate us as we finish our race in victory just as they did.

We are NOT ALONE! Isn't that wonderful?!

"I have fought the good fight, I have finished the race, I have kept the faith."
- 2 Timothy 4:7 ESV

Race Reflections:

Other than Jesus, who is one character in the Bible you would like to have run your race with you? What might they say to encourage you?

(12.1)

THE AFTER-RACE VICTORY CELEBRATION!

Living FROM victory, not FOR victory must be a daily choice. You can't give up. You have to keep running to win!

Would you consider walking from victory? Live FROM and you will win!

I am from Heaven.

I live from Love.

I live from Joy.

I live from Approval.

I live from Provision.

I walk from Power.

I walk from Strength.

I walk from Peace.

I work from Health.

I walk from Victory.

I go from Glory to Glory.

I go from Victory to Victory.

From faith all things are possible!

We are citizens of the Kingdom of God.

Living from Heaven on Earth is our goal! Now go out there and run your own race! We win!

"Therefore, since we are surrounded by so great a cloud of witnesses, let us also lay aside every weight, and sin which clings so closely, and let us run with endurance the race that is set before us, looking to Jesus, the founder and perfecter of our faith, who for the joy that was set before him endured the cross, despising the shame, and is seated at the right hand of the throne of God." - Hebrews 12:1-2 ESV

PRACTICAL TECHNIQUES TO USE EVERYDAY

Create New Thoughts

1. I love myself.

2. I rise daily and prioritize taking care of my spirit, soul, and body first thing in the morning.

3. I am confident in all things.

4. I serve someone every single day with joy.

5. I am decisive and say "yes" or "no" quickly.

6. I am a go-getter.

7. I am forgiven, and my faith saves me.

8. I speak well of everyone.

9. I care for those who are weak.

10. I own things to serve me; things don't own me.

11. I am secure in myself.

12. I am capable to meet every challenge.

13. I am grateful every day.

14. I eat only high quality food.

15. I see the good in everyone.

16. I am a great listener.

17. [Add or replace your own to the list!]

(Your brain does not know what you are currently working for, make the statement to remind yourself. "Neutralize the gunman, secure your perimeters, capture every thought.")

12.1

Create a New Mindset

Directions:

1. Write out what is the current state of your mindset.

   _____

   _____

2. Make a list of what you want it to be instead.

   _____

   _____

   _____

   _____

   _____

   _____

   _____

   _____

3. As you glean ideas about what you need, add those new thoughts to the list above.

4. Make short bullet points of GOOD things that are true in your life right now, and the GOOD things you are going towards.

   -
   -
   -
   -
   -

5. Add at least 50 to 70 details on the list of "New Thoughts."

6. Use your phone to record them (audio or video) and save it.

7. Read the list out loud, and speak slowly, and pause between each line.

8. Every morning and night, replay that audio or video of yourself speaking new habits and beliefs into your life.

Additional journaling space has been provided for you on pages 65-71.

Run Your Day, Don't Let Your Day Run You

What is bothering me? How do I feel stuck? Is it actually true?

1. Item 1

   _____

   _____

2. Item 2

   _____

   _____

3. Item 3

   _____

   _____

What do I desire instead?

1. Desire 1

   _____

   _____

2. Desire 2

   _____

   _____

3. Desire 3

   _____

   _____

Some of the ways I can get there:

1. Path 1

   _____

   _____

2. Path 2

   _____

   _____

3. Path 3

   _____

   _____

(12.1)

SHARE WHY YOU LOVE
12.1 RUN YOUR OWN RACE

As for us, we have all of these great witnesses who encircle us like clouds. So we must let go of every wound that has pierced us and the sin we so easily fall into. Then we will be able to run life's marathon race with passion and determination, for the path has been already marked out before.

- Hebrews 12:1 TPT

After reading Hebrews 12:1, what do you think the 12.1 message is about?

What does this message mean to you?

In 59 seconds or less, share with someone or on social media why you love 12.1 Run Your Own Race.

**Thank you so much for participating in the 12.1 movement.
Let's spread the 12.1 message together!**

Keep Going! Don't Give Up!

(12.1)

MORE ABOUT 12.1 &
HOW YOU CAN GET INVOLVED

12.1 RUN YOUR OWN RACE is a nonprofit organization that serves people who have experienced painful life experiences and loss, and due to their pain no longer enjoy life. We also champion for people who are struggling with debilitating illnesses and diseases, so that they have the emotional support and encouragement they need.

12.1 Run Your Own Race helps people to run life's race with passion and determination. We do this by providing a healing environment and practical techniques to use in everyday life.

Our regional gatherings, community walks, 12.1 races, and workshops provide awareness and a network of support echoing the message of 12.1 Run Your Own Race. Together we are stronger, and we share a message of empowerment, healing, renewal, and strength.

TO RUN OR NOT TO RUN: THAT IS THE QUESTION!

Are you somebody who is looking to run instead of limp through life?

If you want to wake up tomorrow and have joy...

If you want to be emotionally and mentally healthy and thrive...

If you want to be someone who runs your own race with passionate determination...

Then the 12.1 Run Your Own Race movement is for you!

YOU DON'T HAVE TO RUN ALONE

12.1 is "the Facebook® of Kingdom Coaches," connecting hurting people to a community of loving, skilled, and experienced Kingdom runners. Your life's race is your life's process. And we all need a coach to help us run well.

Make a choice today to be surrounded by a great cloud of witnesses/coaches that will walk you through this life's process and achieve the winning results you must have!

CONTACT:

12.1 Run Your Own Race
12.1 Marketing, LLC
Jeanny Rodriguez, Founder

Email: jeanny@12.1runyourownrace.com
Website: www.12.1runyourownrace.com

Facebook: 12.1 Run Your Own Race
Instagram: 12.1_run your own race
Pinterest: 12.1 Run Your Own Race

12.1 MERCHANDISE

Etsy store: https://www.etsy.com/shop/RunYourOwnRace
Shopify: 12.1-Run-your-own-race

Show us your love by wearing one of our awesome t-shirts.
Help us spread the message to Never Give Up!

DONATIONS AND SPONSORSHIPS

The next upcoming event "12.1 We Are One," will help gather people together as friends to celebrate and share their stories of winning beyond tragedy and pain, and how they had breakthrough in their lives and are now "Running Their Own Race." Participants will be provided with valuable connections, community resources, services, personal development opportunities, and free grab bags, and encouraged to consider the possibilities life has to offer. There is joy after loss and pain.

This event will be produced with the help of our local service providers, small business owners, private endorsers, and sponsors. Kindly consider partnering with us and our upcoming "12.1 We Are One" walk. We have a few spaces open for sponsorship opportunities and would love to connect with you!

CONTACT jeanny@12.1runyourownrace.com
DONATE AT paypal.me/121runyourownrace

MISIÓN 12.1 : CORRIENDO TU CARRERA

Una Misión contigo en mente...

Somos un grupo de personas que hemos superado duras pruebas, grandes pérdidas y momentos difíciles en la vida. Es nuestro deseo compartir un mensaje de esperanza, inspiración y superación. Nosotros pudimos vencer momentos duros y proseguir la carrera de nuestra vida, y tú puedes también.

¿Qué es Misión 12.1?

Misión 12.1 es una organización sin fines de lucro cuyo deseo es conectar a las personas que están navegando momentos difíciles en su vida con herramientas necesarias, inspiración, motivación y esperanza. Es nuestro deseo proveerles eventos comunitarios como reuniones regionales, caminatas, y conciertos musicales.

¡El símbolo 12.1 representa tu ganar en la Carrera de Tu Vida!

Por tanto, nosotros también, teniendo en derredor nuestro tan grande nube de testigos, despojémonos de todo peso y del pecado que nos asedia, y corramos con paciencia la carrera que tenemos por delante...
-Hebreos 12:1 (RVR1960)

¿Cómo nos puede ayudar?

Si usted desea unirse a nuestra misión nos puede apoyar hoy al comprar uno de nuestros productos así invitando la conversación de nuestro mensaje de fe y esperanza. Ofrecemos también las siguientes oportunidades para participar:

Únase a nuestra lista de email, y conectese con nosotros en Facebook

Únase a nuestro equipo de palestrantes

Aceptamos invitaciones para Congresos y Eventos Comunitarios

Jeanny Rodriguez, Fundadora

FINAL THOUGHTS FROM JEANNY

Dear Abba,

Thank You!!! You are soooo amazing and awesome.

You are so loving and faithful. You show me so much love and patience. You have waited so long for me to step up and love You like You want and deserve. Here I am thinking my dream is taking sooo long. But You have been waiting for 55 years for me to realize all that You have had for me all this time. You have been waiting a long time for me! I repent for not listening and not running to You much sooner.

Thank You, Abba, for You are so gentle and loving to me. Thank You for taking care of me and providing everything that I need and needed. You are my Provider and my Groom, The Lover of My Soul, Protector, and Defender.

I love You, Jesus. You are the amazing Son of God. Thank You for being my Friend, my Best Friend! You hold my right hand and You never let go. I will walk, serve, wait, and love with You. Today is the best day of my life! I am in Your presence. Help me walk with You every day of my life's race.

Thank You for showing up every time and showing off. Especially today! You are my everything. Thank You for Your Holy Spirit, my Helper. Thank You for praying through me. Thank You, Jesus, for praying for me. Thank You for You live in me. Thank You for all the divine appointments and connections You set up throughout my life. I know...nothing was a fluke or coincidence! Thank You for all the open doors and all the closed doors, too! Thank You for all the joy and sorrow. For all my trials that produce perseverance! The perseverance needed to run my life's race.

Thank you for all my amazing family and my awesome friends!

Please send an extra special blessing to Pedro Adao of 100X, visionary, for believing in 12.1 Run Your Own Race as a movement. Also to Tyler Frick of The King's Company, for his supernatural anointing and connections to You, Abba. To Rachel Newman of Lazarus Tribe Media, for her super-creative gifting and giving heart! To my GREAT cloud of witnesses here on earth...you know who you are! Thank you for crossing lanes with me, pushing me, cheering for me, giving me water when I need it, pulling me, even crying with me! For all the tissues, hugs and kisses...and even the loving, tender smack-downs, too!

—

(12.1)

My prayer is that anyone who reads this work will understand God's perfect plan for their life. That His love passes all understanding, and that you will always remember...

You are never alone!

You are one of a kind!

You are valued!

You are amazing!

You are loved!

I look forward to finishing my life's race well and to hear Him say...

"Well done, good and faithful servant." Matthew 25:21

"Jeanny, you ran my life's race well and I am proud of you..." (I know He will know how to pronounce my name!)

I love you all, but most importantly, today, I want you to know...

Jesus loves you!

Shalom,

Jeanny

(12.1)

TODAY I STAND!

BY JEANNY RODRIGUEZ

Today I stand for the little girl that was not heard...

Today I stand for the little girl that was loved wrong...

Today I stand for the little girl that was hit and was not good enough...

Today I stand for the teenage girl that was afraid and the young woman I let go...

Today I stand for the wife that was betrayed...

Today I stand for the mother who loves too much...

Today I stand because I want to be free!

Today I stand because I am ready to run my own race!

PSALM OF SOLOMON NO. 3

What a lively race!

What a joyous adventure!

To run,

To advance,

In the stride of a Lifetime.

A mirrored glance,

A substanced shadow.

To run,

To dance,

In the stride of a Lifetime.

-From *Psalms of Solomon, Volume I: Poetic Meditations for Worship.* 2019 ©
Rachel Newman. Reprinted with permission.

YOUR RACE STARTS NOW.

RUN WITH PASSION!

STAY IN YOUR LANE.

VICTORY IS ALREADY YOURS!

_____
_____
_____
_____
_____
_____
_____
_____
_____
_____
_____
_____
_____
_____
_____
_____
_____
_____
_____
_____
_____
_____
_____

$$12.1$$

ABOUT THE AUTHOR

Jeanny is a daughter, sister, twin sister, mother, Abu (Abuela), friend, and loving neighbor. She is the founder of the 12.1 Run Your Own Race movement and community. She was born in Santurce, Puerto Rico, moved to upstate New York at the age of 16, has lived in Portugal, and travels extensively. She now lives in a bird sanctuary on a two-mile island off the west coast of Florida. Inspiring people to run their life's race and never give up is her passion. She loves serving and connecting with people. Her favorite things to do are spending time with God and with her loved ones, writing in her gratitude journals, and travel and go walking on the beach.

In her words:

In my life's race I have often asked myself...

Why? Why? Why?

Why me?

This is the question that most comes up in tough times (sound familiar?).

God said...

Count it all joy...

Consider it a blessing...

My Conclusion:

Why not me?! He suffered more than I will ever suffer. I focus on Jesus and I win!

Therefore, my crown is beautiful! This is how I choose to run my race!

My Life's Race Lanes:

> Alcoholism & Addiction
>
> Chronic disease
>
> Poverty
>
> Divorce
>
> Abuse
>
> Adultery
>
> Loss of a child
>
> Loss of a sister (twin) to cancer, and the grief that follows
>
> Cancer survivor

Victory is my only choice!

My hope is that you will join this 12.1 movement of victory. A community choosing to live with our Core Values of Love, Joy, Passion, and Determination.

Never give up! I believe in you!

(12.1)